Behind Closed Doors

Contents

**A darkness done during the
day or the dark of night
Behind Closed Doors:
Molestation**

Chapter 1

Vanessa

Vanessa Williams wrote a book that contained a revelation that she was molested when she was 10 years old.

She was molested by an 18 year old girl who told her to come to her bed.

Vanessa said it felt good that's why she didn't think it was wrong.

But, Vanessa became hypersexual. Because of this she had an abortion in high school.

Stephanie X

Stephanie X appearing on a Spanish court show says she was molested by her stepfather for 5 years.

She went into stripping to support her daughter, all the while suffering from postpartum.

She didn't want her daughter exposed to any men so the same thing wouldn't happen to her daughter.

She was fighting to have sole custody from the biological father of her daughter.

My Experience

I was molested when I was 10 yrs old.

I lived down the street from my molester. My molester was my father figure and friend. I used to sit for hours and listen to the tales of his youth.

My father was absent from my youth, preferring a bottle of whisky to my company.

One night my mother allowed me to spend the night with my friend and his wife. I was so excited. We had dinner and watched some basketball.

Into the evening, his wife excused herself to get ready for bed. His wife went into the shower. He started to get close to me. He sat *really* close to me on the couch.

In the middle of the night, when I was asleep, he came to the couch I was sleeping on and he molested me by touching my genitals and touching my breasts underneath my clothes. I awoke and froze not knowing what to do.

What seemed an eternity, in reality was a few minutes. This happened only once, but its effects have lasted throughout my lifetime.

Years later, when I had my daughter, I was afraid my husband would molest her. I believe this to be a knee-jerk reaction to my molestation.

It was at this time that I began my quest to find answers as to why my trusted friend had betrayed me.

Behind Closed Doors:
Living with the Effects of Molestation

Chapter 2

My Monster

I went to my molester after my daughter was born seeking answers.

I asked him why he had done that to me; touched me that way. His response was complete shock that I had been awake.

His pleasure was my grief. He thought he did the damage without my knowledge. "No", I told him, "I was awake."

He responded with embarrassment that slowly turned into a gruesome chuckle. He told me it was perfectly acceptable in some cultures.

I got up and quietly said, "Not in this culture".

I walked out of his house realizing there had been another side to my friend. He was truly a monster.

The Fallout

Chapter 3

More times than not, there is some type of fallout from being molested that follows the victim throughout their life.

Overcompensating

Overcompensating so as not to draw attention to oneself. Trying to fix every situation; trying to make everyone happy.

Change in personality

Change in personality: becoming shy, retreating and hyper-alert; or the opposite becoming wild, confrontational, and outspoken.

Hyper- sexuality

It is possible to turn to prostitution, stripping, or hyper-sexuality.

These acts all involve a lack of emotion and a distancing oneself sexually from the molestation act that had been experienced.

Fear of your child being molested

Fear that your son or daughter will be molested by your husband, boyfriend, or mate.

Starting fights needlessly so there is a disruption and the child goes with you.

Sleeping with the lights on

Sleeping with the lights on for comfort.

This is a psychological protection against the molester, to 'shine a light' on him or her so he won't perpetrate another crime.

Fear of self

Fear of what you are capable of: Suicide, cutting, alcoholism and drug abuse.

Ironically, fear of what you may do to a child; fear that you will molest and keep the cycle active.

Abortion

For any or all of the aforementioned reasons.

A darkness done during the day
Behind Closed Doors:
Abortion

Chapter 4

Several years ago for 7 days I was in a mental hospital. I believe I got there as a direct result of an abortion I had and the events that followed this abortion.

In the summer, while working at the mall, I met my husband. We dated and after 6 months became physically intimate. We became engaged and it was during the time of our engagement that I became pregnant.

I'll never forget the panic, sheer fear, I felt at the time even though I loved this man very much. I felt so scared at the thought of being 19 years old and becoming a mother.

I'll also never forget my mother's tears and the pain in her eyes as she asked me, "Where did I go wrong?" after I told her of my predicament.

The Wedding

My husband and I decided to get married in Reno, Nevada, in the fall. Six months later we were married in the Catholic Church, three months before the birth of my daughter.

Postpartum Depression

After giving birth, I went through postpartum depression.

Postpartum depression is a condition that some women go through, though not all after giving birth.

After childbirth, the body can go through physical changes that affect the emotions for a period of time. Postpartum usually lasts from months to about a year. My depression never really lifted.

It was at this time I revealed to my husband that I had been molested when I was 10 years old. All of the fallout symptoms (Chapter 3) had one way or another played out in my life.

I paid a visit to my molester (Chapter 2) in desperation for psychological relief. I came home empty.

I even sought counseling. I was told I wanted to sleep with my father. Another dead end.

I was too confused and exhausted from the depression to find another counselor at that time.

Unwanted Pregnancies

Two years later, I became pregnant with my second child. I didn't welcome another child.

I was having a really tough time raising my daughter. The mood swings and depression were intolerable. The postpartum depression was really frightening and confusing for my husband and I.

I had a really hard time taking care of and bonding with my daughter. We didn't think we could go through that ordeal again with another child. So we decided to have an abortion.

The gynecologist I was seeing was pro-choice. Considering all of my circumstances, he persuaded me to make my decision to end the life of my child.

Give your baby and yourself a fighting chance and seek out a pro-life doctor. It will be at a crucial time like this that your doctor can save the life of your child, even when you are too confused or scared to make the decision for life.

Right before the abortion, when I was on the operating table, my pro-choice doctor said to me, "Think about Hawaii" as I fell off to sleep. Imagine. Think about Hawaii as I killed my child.

This would later come back to haunt me.

Coping

At first I felt tremendous relief after the abortion, but then within a very short period of time, I began to feel awful.

I tried to block out the pain through excessive dieting, exercise, drinking and partying.

I also made a feeble attempt at confession.

Unfortunately, I couldn't take the priest's words or the absolution being offered to me to heart.

The guilt remained overwhelming.

Revisiting a Decision

Two years later, in the springtime, amidst a lot of drinking and partying, because of the grief I was experiencing from the first abortion, I sought my second abortion.

I reasoned that I was going to hell anyway as a direct result of not believing that God could ever forgive me.

This time, instead of going back to my gynecologist, I went to the local Family Planning Clinic.

It was here that I was welcomed with open arms with my decision to have an abortion. I was never persuaded to seek an abortion alternative.

I vividly remember the routineness of the pre-abortion procedure as I awaited my turn to end the life of my child.

Sitting on the bench in the pre-op waiting room, I was joined by two other girls who giggled as they watched their favorite soap opera.

I kept thinking just another day; just another murder. But these murders aren't publicized on the evening news. These children die in the silence of their mother's wombs.

There are no sensationalized murder trials, there is no cry for justice, and there are no jury decisions for life imprisonment for these murders.

There is a greater and farther reaching justice that begins in the heart and life of the woman who decides to murder her child the day she takes its life.

The Fear

After this second abortion I felt an overwhelming fear that I actually was going to go to hell.

So I 'bargained' with God in the only way I knew how. I had my fallopian tubes tied. It was my ignorant way of proving to God that I would never have another abortion ever again.

But you can't barter evil for evil. I was killing a part of my body by having a tubal ligation; throwing my body further out of balance.

My Third Pregnancy

Three years after the tubal ligation and as a direct result of it, I had an ectopic pregnancy.

I was shopping in the mall and felt a sudden stabbing pain below my stomach. My husband was with me. He put me in the car and I was rushed to the hospital.

My fallopian tube had blown up inside of me. I was hemorrhaging. I had lost yet another child.

Gradual Descent

Remember the post partum depression I had referred to earlier after the birth of my daughter? That was nothing compared to the downward turn my health began to take both emotionally and physically.

My mood swings were horrendous. I once again tried to exercise my way into feeling better. Every day I had to run 5 miles just to feel close to being human.

By this time, my hormones were becoming depleted in my body due to the tubal ligation.

This, coupled with the tremendous guilt I felt, made my situation more than I could bear.

The Experience

In all, this gradual descent into my hellish experience took roughly 7 years and culminated in my actually believing I was in hell.

I had a psychotic break. In my mind I really didn't know if I had died and gone to hell or was still here on earth.

Everything around me looked the same, but nothing felt the same. I couldn't connect.

The worst part of it all was that I couldn't feel the presence of God. I felt completely alone.

I was in constant, terrifying fear. I couldn't sleep for days. My peace was gone.

Instead of the blue islands of Hawaii promised to me by my pro-choice gynecologist who had performed my first abortion, I had bargained for the depths of hell.

Institutionalization

I was admitted to a mental hospital by my family.

It wouldn't have mattered where I was because the hell going on inside of me couldn't be contained within the hospital walls. The breakdown consumed me.

It took a caring family, a tremendous amount of prayer on their part and several long, agonizing years of trying different psychiatric medications, vitamin therapy, and very painful hormone shots to become mentally stable.

Project Rachel

When I stabilized, I sought out counseling for my deep internal, psychological pain.

I had heard about the Project Rachel program several times through my church.

It is a counseling and healing service provided by people who have had abortions or people who were trained to help those in post abortion crisis.

I was blessed to be taken in and counseled.

Through Project Rachel I named, honored, and said 'goodbye' to my children with the help of my parish priest in the springtime.

Renewal

I sought and obtained the reversal of my tubal ligation for my one remaining fallopian tube one year later at a cost of $6,000.

I gradually began to feel God's presence in my life again.

I know I am alive and functioning only because of God's enormously generous mercy and forgiveness.

What I have been through was beyond my wildest dreams of what hell could be. Coming out of it is an undeserved miracle.

Conclusion

Not all molestations end in the woman seeking out an abortion. But I believe there is an acknowledgeable amount of women who do.

Would my life have turned out differently without the molestation experience? I am convinced it would have.

I am convinced the victim of molestation experiences fallout for each act of molestation.   Mine culminated in abortion and mental health issues.

To all of you out there who have faced the horror of molestation and/or abortion I urge you to bring what happened to you out in the open for healing and out from Behind Closed Doors.

Resources

Child Molestation Prevention
(Sources for Counseling)
www.childmolestationprevention.org

Right to Life League
www.nrlc.org

Project Rachel
www.hopeafterabortion.com

Notes

Notes